Mom

I hope you enjoy the reading in this book. My Mother had one and really liked it.

Love,
Jill
6-2002

W9-BDS-731

To:

Mom

From:

Juli

The Helen Steiner Rice Foundation

When someone does a kindness
it always seems to me
That's the way God up in heaven
would like us all to be . . .

Whatever the celebration, whatever the day, whatever the event, whatever the occasion, Helen Steiner Rice possessed the ability to express the appropriate feeling for that particular moment. A happening became happier, a sentiment more sentimental, a memory more memorable because of her deep sensitivity and ability to put into understandable language the emotion being experienced. Her positive attitude, her concern for others, and her love of God are identifiable threads woven into her life, her work . . . and even her death.

Prior to Mrs. Rice's passing, she established the Helen Steiner Rice Foundation, a nonprofit corporation that awards grants to worthy charitable programs assisting the elderly and the needy.

Royalties from the sale of this book will add to the financial capabilities of the Helen Steiner Rice Foundation. Because of limited resources, the foundation presently limits grants to qualified charitable programs in Lorain, Ohio, where Helen Steiner Rice was born, and Greater Cincinnati, Ohio, where Mrs. Rice lived and worked most of her life. Hopefully in the future, resources will be of sufficient size that broader geographical areas may be considered in the awarding of grants.

Because of her foresight, caring, and deep conviction of sharing, Helen Steiner Rice continues to touch a countless number of lives through foundational grants and through her inspirational poetry.

Thank you for your assistance in helping to keep Helen's dream alive and growing.

ANDREA E. CORNETT, ADMINISTRATOR

HEART GIFTS

Helen Steiner Rice

Fleming H. Revell
A Division of Baker Book House Co
Grand Rapids, Michigan 49516

© 1968, 1987, 1999 by Fleming H. Revell
and The Helen Steiner Rice Foundation

Published by Fleming H. Revell
a division of Baker Book House Company
P.O. Box 6287, Grand Rapids, MI 49516-6287

Second printing, July 2000

Printed in the United States of America

All rights reserved. No part of this publication may be reproduced, stored in a retrieval system, or transmitted in any form or by any means—for example, electronic, photocopy, recording—without the prior written permission of the publisher. The only exception is brief quotations in printed reviews.

Library of Congress Cataloging-in-Publication Data

Rice, Helen Steiner.
    [Heart gifts from Helen Steiner Rice]
    Heart gifts / Helen Steiner Rice.
      p.   cm.
    Rev. ed. of: Heart gifts from Helen Steiner Rice. [1968].
    ISBN 0-8007-1767-8
    1. Christian poetry, American. I. Title.
PS3568.I28H4 1999
  811′.54—dc21   99-22032

Interior design by Robin Black.

Research for footnotes on pp. 81–95 was conducted by Virginia Wiltse.

For current information about all releases from Baker Book House, visit our web site:
http://www.bakerbooks.com

*S*how me the way,
    not to fortune and fame,
Not how to win laurels
    or praise for my name—
But show me the way
    to spread the great story
That "Thine is the kingdom
    and power and glory."

Contents

Preface

When we first began publishing the poetry of Helen Steiner Rice, we started with a small collection of verse, handpicked by Helen herself. She titled it *Heart Gifts*, for that's what these poems were: small gifts of poetry from her heart, written to speak to the hearts of her readers.

Published over thirty years ago, *Heart Gifts* has touched hundreds of thousands of lives. We have since published many other collections of Helen's poetry, which have had the same enthusiastic welcome that *Heart Gifts* has had. In fact, her poetry is so well loved around the world that she has come to be known as the "poet laureate of popular verse."

How could one woman make such a profound impact on so many people? One observer said she had "the rare gift of sensing people's fundamental needs, of reaching into their hearts and leaving there a firmer grasp of the lasting realities of faith and hope and love." But she was not satisfied to simply let this gift go undeveloped. Her gifts of insight and wisdom were nurtured by her continual interaction with people in need. She developed long-lasting relationships with the people who responded to her poetry: the heartbroken, the ill, the lonely, and the needy, as well as the rejoicing and hope-filled.

Helen Steiner Rice gloried in the everyday happenings of life. She knew that the people who have the best grasp on life are those who truly understand the ebb and flow of life and who struggle with the day-to-day joys and disappointments of jobs and families: those who rejoice in a baby's first step, a grandchild's crayon picture, a daughter's wedding; those who weep for a father's death or sister's illness; those who count among their most treasured possessions the memories of family and friends.

And these are the people Helen Steiner Rice valued. She sought their company, listened to their laughter, shared their tears. And when she wrote, she wrote for them, giving voice to their thoughts and feelings.

As we began to plan this reissue of *Heart Gifts,* we were struck again with the timelessness of Helen's verse. Her pen was stilled on April 23, 1981, but her words continue to offer comfort and hope to a needy world.

As you read through this volume, first her poems, then her story, "Out of My Life," we hope you will be renewed, refreshed, and encouraged.

THE PUBLISHERS

HEART GIFTS

It's not the things that can be bought
    that are life's richest treasure,
It's just the little "heart gifts"
    that money cannot measure.
A cheerful smile, a friendly word,
    a sympathetic nod
Are priceless little treasures
    from the storehouse of our God.
They are the things that can't be bought
    with silver or with gold,
For thoughtfulness and kindness
    and love are never sold.
They are the priceless things in life
    for which no one can pay,
And the giver finds rich recompense
    in giving them away.

A Sure Way to a Happy Day

Happiness is something
　　we create in our mind,
It's not something we search for
　　and so seldom find—
It's just waking up
　　and beginning the day
By counting our blessings
　　and kneeling to pray—
It's giving up thoughts
　　that breed discontent
And accepting what comes
　　as a "gift heaven-sent"—
It's giving up wishing
　　for things we have not
And making the best of
　　whatever we've got—
It's knowing that life
　　is determined for us,
And pursuing our tasks
　　without fret, fume, or fuss—
For it's by completing
　　what God gives us to do
That we find real contentment
　　and happiness too.

PRAYERS ARE THE STAIRS TO GOD

Prayers are the stairs
   we must climb every day,
If we would reach God
   there is no other way,
For we learn to know God
   when we meet Him in prayer
And ask Him to lighten
   our burden of care.
So start in the morning
   and, though the way's steep,
Climb ever upward
   'til your eyes close in sleep—
For prayers are the stairs
   that lead to the Lord,
And to meet Him in prayer
   is the climber's reward.

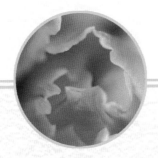

THERE'S SUNSHINE IN A SMILE

Life is a mixture
   of sunshine and rain,
Laughter and pleasure,
   teardrops and pain.
All days can't be bright,
   but it's certainly true,
There was never a cloud
   the sun didn't shine through.
So just keep on smiling
   whatever betide you,
Secure in the knowledge
   God is always beside you,
And you'll find when you smile
   your day will be brighter
And all of your burdens
   will seem so much lighter—
For each time you smile
   you will find it is true,
Somebody, somewhere
   will smile back at you,
And nothing on earth
   can make life more worthwhile
Than the sunshine and warmth
   of a beautiful smile.

WIDEN MY VISION

God, open my eyes
   so I may see
And feel Your presence
   close to me,
Give me strength
   for my stumbling feet
As I battle the crowd
   on life's busy street,
And widen the vision
   of my unseeing eyes
So in passing faces
   I'll recognize
Not just a stranger,
   unloved and unknown,
But a friend with a heart
   that is much like my own.
Give me perception
   to make me aware
That scattered profusely
   on life's thoroughfare
Are the very best gifts
   that we daily pass by
As we look at the world
   with an unseeing eye.

If God Is There

I have prayed on my knees in the morning,
    I have prayed as I walked along,
I have prayed in the silence and darkness
    and I've prayed to the tune of a song—
I have prayed in the midst of triumph
    and I've prayed when I suffered defeat,
I have prayed on the sands of the seashore
    where the waves of the ocean beat—
I have prayed in a velvet-hushed forest
    where the quietness calmed my fears,
I have prayed through suffering and heartache
    when my eyes were blinded with tears—
I have prayed in churches and chapels,
    cathedrals and synagogues too,
But often I've had the feeling
    that my prayers were not getting through.

And I realized then that our Father
    is not really concerned *where* we pray
Or impressed by our manner of worship
    or the eloquent words that we say,
He is only concerned with our feelings,
    and He looks deep into our heart
And hears the "cry of our soul's deep need"
    that no words could ever impart.
So it isn't the prayer that's expressive
    or offered in some special spot,
It's the sincere plea of a sinner
    and God can tell whether or not
We honestly seek His forgiveness
    and earnestly mean what we say,
And then and then only, He answers
    the prayer that we fervently pray.

WHERE CAN WE FIND HIM?

Where can we find the Holy One?
Where can we see His only Son?
The wise men asked, and we're asking still,
Where can we find this man of goodwill?
Is He far away in some distant place,
Ruling unseen from His throne of grace?
Is there nothing on earth that we can see
To give us proof of eternity?
It's true we have never looked on His face,
But His likeness shines forth from every place,
For the hand of God is everywhere
Along life's busy thoroughfare,

And His presence can be felt and seen
Right in the midst of our daily routine.
The things we touch and see and feel
Are what make God so very real—
The silent stars in timeless skies,
The wonderment in a child's eyes,
The gossamer wings of a hummingbird,
The joy that comes from a kindly word,
The autumn haze, the breath of spring,
The chirping song the crickets sing,
A rosebud in a slender vase,
A smile upon a friendly face . . .
In everything both great and small,
We see the hand of God in all,
And every day, somewhere, someplace,
We see the likeness of His face,
For who can watch a new day's birth
Or touch the warm, life-giving earth,
Or feel the softness of the breeze,
Or look at skies through lacy trees
And say they've never seen His face
Or looked upon His throne of grace?

$\mathscr{G}$OD IS NEVER
BEYOND OUR REACH

No one ever sought the Father
　and found He was not there,
And no burden is too heavy
　to be lightened by a prayer.
No problem is too intricate
　and no sorrow that we face
Is too deep and devastating
　to be softened by His grace.
No trials and tribulations
　are beyond what we can bear
If we can share them with our Father
　as we talk to Him in prayer—

And people of every color,
    every race, and every creed
Have but to seek the Father
    in their deepest hour of need.
God asks for no credentials,
    He accepts us with our flaws,
He is kind and understanding
    and He welcomes us because
We are His erring children
    and He loves us every one,
And He freely and completely
    forgives all that we've done,
Asking only if we're ready
    to follow where He leads—
Content that in His wisdom
    He will answer all our needs.

THE PEACE
OF MEDITATION

So we may know God better
    and feel His quiet power,
Let us daily keep in silence
    a meditation hour—
For to understand God's greatness
    and to use His gifts each day
The soul must learn to meet Him
    in a meditative way,
For our Father tells His children
    that if they would know His will
They must seek Him in the silence
    when all is calm and still . . .
For nature's greatest forces
    are found in quiet things
Like softly falling snowflakes
    drifting down on angels' wings,
Or petals dropping soundlessly
    from a lovely full-blown rose,

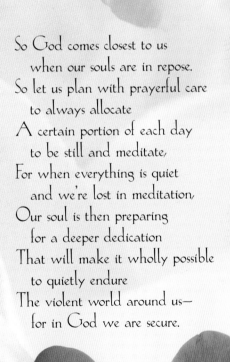

So God comes closest to us
   when our souls are in repose.
So let us plan with prayerful care
   to always allocate
A certain portion of each day
   to be still and meditate,
For when everything is quiet
   and we're lost in meditation,
Our soul is then preparing
   for a deeper dedication
That will make it wholly possible
   to quietly endure
The violent world around us—
   for in God we are secure.

THANK GOD
FOR LITTLE THINGS

Thank You, God, for little things
    that often come our way,
The things we take for granted
    but don't mention when we pray—
The unexpected courtesy,
    the thoughtful, kindly deed,
A hand reached out to help us
    in our time of sudden need—
Oh, make us more aware, dear God,
    of little daily graces
That come to us with "sweet surprise"
    from never-dreamed-of places.

QUIT SUPPOSIN'

Don't start your day by supposin'
   that trouble is just ahead,
It's better to stop supposin'
   and start with a prayer instead.
And make it a prayer of thanksgiving
   for the wonderful things God has wrought
Like the beautiful sunrise and sunset,
   God's gifts that are free and not bought.
For what is the use of supposin'
   the dire things that could happen to you
And worrying about some misfortune
   that seldom if every comes true.
But instead of just idle supposin'
   step forward to meet each new day
Secure in the knowledge God's near you
   to lead you each step of the way—
For supposin' the worst things will happen
   only helps to make them come true,
And you darken the bright, happy moments
   that the dear Lord has given to you.
So if you desire to be happy
   and get rid of the misery of dread
Just give up supposin' the worst things
   and look for the best things instead.

God Is Our Encouragement

Sometimes we feel uncertain
  and unsure of everything,
Afraid to make decisions,
  dreading what the day will bring.
We keep wishing it were possible
  to dispel all fear and doubt
And to understand more readily
  just what life is all about.
God has given us the answers,
  which too often go unheeded,
But if we search His promises
  we'll find everything that's needed
To lift our faltering spirits
  and renew our courage too,
For there's absolutely nothing
  too much for God to do—
For the Lord is our salvation
  and our strength in every fight,
Our redeemer and protector,
  our eternal guiding light.

He has promised to sustain us,
   He's our refuge from all harms,
And underneath this refuge
   are the everlasting arms.
So cast your burden on Him,
   seek His counsel when distressed,
And go to Him for comfort
   when you're lonely and oppressed.
For God is our encouragement
   in trouble and in trials,
And in suffering and in sorrow
   He will turn our tears to smiles.

NEVER BORROW SORROW FROM TOMORROW

Deal only with the present,
    never step into tomorrow,
For God asks us just to trust Him
    and to never borrow sorrow—
For the future is not ours to know,
    and it may never be,
So let us live and give our best
    and give it lavishly,
For to meet tomorrow's troubles
    before they are even ours
Is to anticipate the Savior
    and to doubt His all-wise powers.
So let us be content to solve
    our problems one by one,
Asking nothing of tomorrow
    except "Thy will be done."

GOD'S JEWELS

We watch the rich and famous
   bedecked in precious jewels,
Enjoying earthly pleasures,
   defying moral rules—
And in our mood of discontent
   we sink into despair
And long for earthly riches
   and feel cheated of our share.
But stop these idle musings,
   God has stored up for you
Treasures that are far beyond
   earth's jewels and riches too.
For never, never discount
   what God has promised man
If he will walk in meekness
   and accept God's flawless plan—
For if we heed His teachings
   as we journey through the years,
We'll find the richest jewels of all
   are crystalized from tears.

Unaware,
We Pass Him By

On life's busy thoroughfares
We meet with angels unawares—
But we are too busy to listen or hear,
Too busy to sense that God is near,
Too busy to stop and recognize
The grief that lies in another's eyes,
Too busy to offer to help or share,
Too busy to sympathize or care,
Too busy to do the good things we should,
Telling ourselves we would if we could . . .
But life is too swift and the pace is too great
And we dare not pause for we might be late
For our next appointment, which means so much
We are willing to brush off the Savior's touch,
And we tell ourselves there will come a day
We will have more time to pause on our way . . .
But before we know it life's sun has set
And we've passed the Savior but never met,
For hurrying along life's thoroughfare
We passed Him by and remained unaware
That within the very sight of our eye,
Unnoticed, the Son of God passed by.

"This Too Will Pass Away"

If I can endure for this minute
    whatever is happening to me,
No matter how heavy my heart is
    or how dark the moment may be—
If I can remain calm and quiet
    with all my world crashing about me,
Secure in the knowledge God loves me
    when everyone else seems to doubt me—
If I can but keep on believing
    what I know in my heart to be true,
That darkness will fade with the morning
    and that this will pass away too—
Then nothing in life can defeat me
    for as long as this knowledge remains
I can suffer whatever is happening
    for I know God will break all the chains
That are binding me tight in the darkness
    and trying to fill me with fear,
For there is no night without dawning,
    and I know that my morning is near.

TROUBLE IS A STEPPING-STONE TO GROWTH

Trouble is something no one can escape,
Everyone has it in some form or shape—
Some people hide it way down deep inside,
Some people bear it with gallant-like pride,
Some people worry and complain of their lot,
Some people covet what they haven't got,
While others rebel and become bitter and old
With hopes that are dead and hearts that are cold.
But the wise men accept whatever God sends,
Willing to yield like a storm-tossed tree bends,
Knowing that God never makes a mistake,
So whatever He sends they are willing to take.
For trouble is part and parcel of life
And no one can grow without trouble and strife,
And the steep hills ahead and high mountain peaks
Afford us at last the peace that we seek.
So blest are the people who learn to accept
The trouble we try to escape and reject,
For in our acceptance we're given great grace
And courage and faith and the strength to face
The daily troubles that come to us all
So we may learn to stand straight and tall—
For the grandeur of life is born of defeat
For in overcoming we make life complete.

FATHERS ARE WONDERFUL PEOPLE

Fathers are wonderful people,
  too little understood,
And we do not sing their praises
  as often as we should,
For somehow Father seems to be
  the man who pays the bills,
While Mother binds up little hurts
  and nurses all our ills.
And Father struggles daily
  to live up to his image
As protector and provider
  and "hero of the scrimmage,"
And perhaps that is the reason
  we sometimes get the notion
That Fathers are not subject
  to the thing we call emotion.

But if you look inside Dad's heart,
   where no one else can see,
You'll find he's sentimental
   and as soft as he can be,
But he's so busy every day
   in the grueling race of life,
He leaves the sentimental stuff
   to his partner and his wife.
But Fathers are just wonderful
   in a million different ways,
And they merit loving compliments
   and accolades of praise,
For the only reason Dad aspires
   to fortune and success
Is to make the family proud of him
   and to bring them happiness,
And like our heavenly Father,
   he's a guardian and a guide,
Someone we can count on
   to be always on our side.

A TRIBUTE TO DAUGHTERS

Every home should have a daughter,
    for there's nothing like a girl
To keep the world around her
    in one continuous whirl.
She is soft and sweet and cuddly,
    but she's also wise and smart,
She's a wondrous combination
    of a mind and brain and heart.
And even in her baby days
    she's just a born coquette,
And anything she really wants
    she manages to get,

For even at a tender age
    she uses all her wiles,
And she can melt the hardest heart
    with the sunshine of her smiles.
She starts out as a rosebud
    with her beauty unrevealed,
Then through a happy childhood
    her petals are unsealed . . .
She's soon a sweet girl graduate,
    and then a blushing bride,
And then a lovely woman
    as the rosebud opens wide . . .
And some day in the future,
    if it be God's gracious will,
She, too, will be a mother
    and know that reverent thrill
That comes to every mother
    whose heart is filled with love
When she beholds the "angel"
    that God sent her from above,
And there would be no life at all
    in this world or the other
Without a darling daughter
    who, in turn, becomes a mother!

A Prayer
for the Young

Dear God, I keep praying
    for the things I desire,
You tell me I'm selfish
    and playing with fire—
It is hard to believe
    I am selfish and vain,
My desires seem so real
    and my needs seem so sane.
And yet You are wiser
    and Your vision is wide
And You look down on me
    and You see deep inside.
You know it's so easy
    to change and distort,
And things that are evil
    seem so harmless a sport.
Oh, teach me, dear God,
    to not rush ahead
But to pray for Your guidance
    and to trust You instead,
For You know what I need
    and that I'm only a slave
To the things that I want
    and desire and crave.

Oh, God, in your mercy
   look down on me now
And see in my heart
   that I love You somehow,
Although in my rashness,
   impatience, and greed,
I pray for the things
   that I want and don't need—
And instead of a crown
   please send me a cross
And teach me to know
   that all gain is but loss,
And show me the way
   to joy without end,
With You as my Father,
   Redeemer, and Friend,
And send me the things
   that are hardest to bear,
And keep me forever
   safe in Your care.

WHEN TROUBLE COMES

Let us go quietly to God
 when troubles come to us,
Let us never stop to whimper
 or complain and fret and fuss,
Let us hide our thorns in roses
 and our sighs in golden song
And our crosses in a crown of smiles
 whenever things go wrong . . .
For no one can really help us
 as our troubles we bemoan,
For comfort, help, and inner peace
 must come from God alone.
So do not tell your neighbor,
 your companion, or your friend
In the hope that they can help you
 bring your troubles to an end,

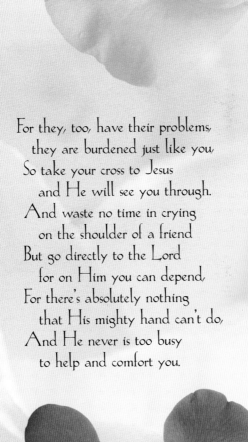

For they, too, have their problems,
   they are burdened just like you,
So take your cross to Jesus
   and He will see you through.
And waste no time in crying
   on the shoulder of a friend
But go directly to the Lord
   for on Him you can depend,
For there's absolutely nothing
   that His mighty hand can't do,
And He never is too busy
   to help and comfort you.

More of Thee...
Less of Me

Take me and break me and make me, dear God,
   just what You want me to be,
Give me the strength to accept what You send
   and eyes with the vision to see
All the small arrogant ways that I have
   and the vain little things that I do,
Make me aware that I'm often concerned
   more with myself than with You.
Uncover before me my weakness and greed
   and help me to search deep inside
So I may discover how easy it is
   to be selfishly lost in my pride.
And then in Your goodness and mercy
   look down on this weak, erring one
And tell me that I am forgiven
   for all I've so willfully done,
And teach me to humbly start following
   the path that the dear Savior trod
So I'll find at the end of life's journey
   a home in the city of God!

GOD'S HAND

Everywhere across the land
You see God's face and touch His hand.
Each time you look up in the sky
Or watch the fluffy clouds drift by,
Or feel the sunshine warm and bright,
Or watch the dark night turn to light,
Or hear a bluebird gaily sing,
Or see the winter turn to spring,
Or stop to pick a daffodil,
Or gather violets on some hill,
Or touch a leaf or see a tree,
It's all God whispering, "This is Me,
And I am faith and I am light,
And in Me there shall be no night."

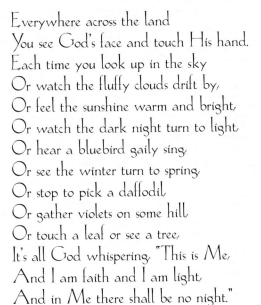

DAILY PRAYERS
DISSOLVE YOUR CARES

I meet God in the morning
   and go with Him through the day,
Then in the stillness of the night
   before sleep comes I pray
That God will just take over
   all the problems I couldn't solve
And in the peacefulness of sleep
   my cares will all dissolve,
So when I open up my eyes
   to greet another day
I'll find myself renewed in strength
   and there'll open up a way
To meet what seemed impossible
   for me to solve alone
And once again I'll be assured
   I am never on my own.
For if we try to stand alone,
   we are weak and we will fall,
For God is always greatest
   when we're helpless, lost, and small.
And no day is unmeetable
   if on rising our first thought
Is to thank God for the blessings
   that His loving care has brought,

For there can be no failures
    or hopeless, unsaved sinners
If we enlist the help of God
    Who makes all losers winners.
So meet Him in the morning
    and go with Him through the day
And thank Him for His guidance
    each evening when you pray,
And if you follow faithfully
    this daily way to pray,
You will never in your lifetime
    face another hopeless day.

No Prayer
Goes Unheard

Often we pause and wonder
    when we kneel down to pray,
Can God really hear
    the prayers that we say . . .
But if we keep praying
    and talking to Him,
He'll brighten the soul
    that was clouded and dim,
And as we continue,
    our burden seems lighter,
Our sorrow is softened
    and our outlook is brighter,
For though we feel helpless
    and alone when we start,
Our prayer is the key
    that opens the heart,
And as our heart opens
    the dear Lord comes in
And the prayer that we felt
    we could never begin
Is so easy to say
    for the Lord understands
And gives us new strength
    by the touch of His hands.

BEFORE YOU CAN DRY ANOTHER'S TEARS

Let me not live a life that's free
From the things that draw me close to Thee,
For how can I ever hope to heal
The wounds of others I do not feel?
If my eyes are dry and I never weep,
How do I know when the hurt is deep?
If my heart is cold and it never bleeds,
How can I tell what my brother needs?
For when ears are deaf to the beggar's plea
And we close our eyes and refuse to see
And we steel our hearts and harden our mind
And we count it a weakness whenever we're kind,
We are no longer following the Father's way
Or seeking His guidance from day to day—
For without crosses to carry and burdens to bear,
We dance through a life that is frothy and fair,
And chasing the rainbow we have no desire
For roads that are rough and realms that are higher.
So spare me no heartache or sorrow, dear Lord,
For the heart that is hurt reaps the richest reward,
And God enters the heart that is broken with sorrow
As He opens the door to a brighter tomorrow,
For only through tears can we recognize
The suffering that lies in another's eyes.

THE DIFFERENCE BETWEEN "DRIVE" AND "DRIVEN"

There's a difference between "drive" and "driven"—
The one is selfish the other God-given.
For the driven man has but one goal,
Just wordly wealth and not riches of soul,
And daily he's spurred on to reach and attain
A higher position, more profit and gain,
Ambition and wealth become his great need
As daily he's driven by avarice and greed.
But most blessed are they who use their drive
To work with zeal so all may survive,
For while they forfeit great personal gain,
Their work and their zeal are never in vain,
For they contribute to the whole human race,
And we cannot survive without growing in grace.
So help us, dear God, to choose between
The driving forces that rule our routine
So we may make our purpose and goal
Not power and wealth but the growth of our soul,
And give us strength and drive and desire
To raise our standards and ethics higher
So all of us and not just a few
May live on earth as You want us to.

Prayers Can't Be Answered Unless They Are Prayed

Life without purpose is barren indeed—
There can't be a harvest unless you plant seed,
There can't be attainment unless there's a goal,
And man's but a robot unless there's a soul.
If we send no ships out, no ships will come in,
And unless there's a contest, nobody can win,
For games can't be won unless they are played,
And prayers can't be answered unless they are prayed.
So whatever is wrong with your life today,
You'll find a solution if you kneel down and pray
Not just for pleasure, enjoyment, and health,
Not just for honors and prestige and wealth,
But pray for a purpose to make life worth living,
And pray for the joy of unselfish giving,
For great is your gladness and rich your reward
When you make your life's purpose the choice of the Lord.

THE Way TO GOD

If my days were untroubled
  and my heart always light
Would I seek that fair land
  where there is no night?
If I never grew weary
  with the weight of my load
Would I search for God's peace
  at the end of the road?
If I never knew sickness
  and never felt pain
Would I reach for a hand
  to help and sustain?
If I walked not with sorrow
  and lived without loss
Would my soul seek sweet solace
  at the foot of the cross?
If all I desired was mine
  day by day
Would I kneel before God
  and earnestly pray?

If God sent no winter
    to freeze me with fear
Would I yearn for the warmth
    of spring every year?
I ask myself this
    and the answer is plain—
If my life were all pleasure
    and I never knew pain
I'd seek God less often
    and need Him much less,
For God's sought more often
    in times of distress,
And no one knows God
    or sees Him as plain
As those who have met Him
    on the pathway of pain.

GOD BLESS AMERICA

"America the beautiful"—
    may it always stay that way—
But to keep Old Glory flying
    there's a price that we must pay,
For everything worth having
    demands work and sacrifice,
And freedom is a gift from God
    that commands the highest price.
For all our wealth and progress
    are as worthless as can be
Without the faith that made us great
    and kept our country free,
Nor can our nation hope to live
    unto itself alone,
For the problems of our neighbors
    must today become our own.

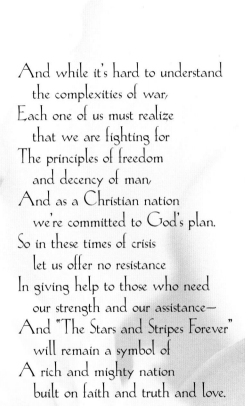

And while it's hard to understand
   the complexities of war,
Each one of us must realize
   that we are fighting for
The principles of freedom
   and decency of man,
And as a Christian nation
   we're committed to God's plan.
So in these times of crisis
   let us offer no resistance
In giving help to those who need
   our strength and our assistance—
And "The Stars and Stripes Forever"
   will remain a symbol of
A rich and mighty nation
   built on faith and truth and love.

WARM OUR HEARTS
WITH YOUR LOVE

Oh, God, who made the summer
    and warmed the earth with beauty,
Warm our hearts with gratitude
    and devotion to our duty,
For in this age of violence,
    rebellion, and defiance,
We've forgotten the true meaning
    of dependable reliance.
We have lost our sense of duty
    and our sense of values too,
And what was once unsanctioned,
    no longer is taboo.

Our standards have been lowered,
and we resist all discipline,
And our vision has been narrowed
and blinded to all sin.
Oh, put the summer brightness
in our closed, unseeing eyes
So in the careworn faces
that we pass we'll recognize
The heartbreak and the loneliness,
the trouble and despair
That a word of understanding
would make easier to bear.
Oh, God, look down on our cold hearts
and warm them with Your love,
And grant us Your forgiveness,
which we're so unworthy of.

Count Your Gains
and Not Your Losses

As we travel down life's busy road
Complaining of our heavy load,
We often think God's been unfair
And given us more than our share
Of little daily irritations
And disappointing tribulations.
We're discontented with our lot
And all the bad breaks that we got,
We count our losses, not our gain,
And remember only tears and pain.
And wrapped up in our own despair
We have no time to see or share
Another's load that far outweighs
Our little problems and dismays.
And so we walk with head held low
And little do we guess or know
That someone near us on life's street
Is burdened deeply with defeat.
But if we'd but forget our care
And stop in sympathy to share
The burden that our brother carried,
Our mind and heart would be less harried,
And we would feel our load was small,
In fact, we carried no load at all.

BIRTHDAYS ARE
A GIFT FROM GOD

Where does time go in its endless flight—
Spring turns to fall and day to night,
And birthdays come and birthdays go
And where they go we do not know.
But God who planned our life on earth
And gave our mind and body birth
And then enclosed a living soul
With heaven as the spirit's goal
Has given us the gift of choice
To follow that small inner voice
That speaks to us from year to year
Reminding us we've naught to fear,
For birthdays are a stepping-stone
To endless joys as yet unknown.
So fill each day with happy things
And may your burdens all take wings
And fly away and leave behind
Great joy of heart and peace of mind,
For birthdays are the gateway to
An endless life of joy for you
If you but pray from day to day
That He will show you the truth and the way.

God Knows Best

Our Father knows what's best for us,
   so why should we complain—
We always want the sunshine,
   but He knows there must be rain.
We love the sound of laughter
   and the merriment of cheer,
But our hearts would lose their tenderness
   if we never shed a tear.
Our Father tests us often
   with suffering and with sorrow,
He tests us, not to punish us,
   but to help us meet tomorrow,
For growing trees are strengthened
   when they withstand the storm,

And the sharp cut of the chisel
    gives the marble grace and form.
God never hurts us needlessly,
    and He never wastes our pain,
For every loss He sends to us
    is followed by rich gain,
And when we count the blessings
    that God has so freely sent,
We will find no cause for murmuring
    and no time to lament,
For our Father loves His children,
    and to Him all things are plain,
So He never sends us pleasure
    when the soul's deep need is pain.
So whenever we are troubled,
    and when everything goes wrong,
It is just God working in us
    to make our spirit strong.

My God Is No Stranger

I've never seen God,
    but I know how I feel,
It's people like you
    who make Him so real.
My God is no stranger,
    He's friendly and gay,
And He doesn't ask me
    to weep when I pray.
It seems that I pass Him
    so often each day
In the faces of people
    I meet on my way.
He's the stars in the heaven,
    a smile on some face,
A leaf on a tree
    or a rose in a vase,
He's winter and autumn
    and summer and spring,
In short, God is every
    real, wonderful thing.
I wish I might meet Him
    much more than I do—
I would if there were
    more people like you.

WHY SHOULD HE DIE
FOR SUCH AS I?

In everything both great and small
We see the hand of God in all,
And in the miracles of spring
When everywhere in everything
His handiwork is all around
And every lovely sight and sound
Proclaims the God of earth and sky
I ask myself, "Just who am I
That God should send His only Son
That my salvation would be won
Upon a cross by a sinless man
To bring fulfillment to God's plan?"
For Jesus suffered, bled, and died
That sinners might be sanctified,
And to grant God's children such as I
Eternal life in that home on high.

THE SEASONS
OF THE SOUL

Why am I cast down
   and despondently sad
When I long to be happy
   and joyous and glad?
Why is my heart heavy
   with unfathomable weight
As I try to escape
   this soul-saddened state?
I ask myself often,
   "What makes life this way,
Why is the song silenced
   in the heart that was gay?"
And then with God's help
   it all becomes clear,
The soul has its seasons
   just the same as the year—
I too must pass through
   life's autumn of dying,
A desolate period
   of heart-hurt and crying,
Followed by winter
   in whose frostbitten hand
My heart is as frozen
   as the snow-covered land.

Yes, we too must pass through
    the seasons God sends,
Content in the knowledge
    that everything ends,
And oh what a blessing
    to know there are reasons
And to find that our soul
    must, too, have its seasons—
Bounteous seasons
    and barren ones too,
Times for rejoicing
    and times to be blue—
But meeting these seasons
    of dark desolation
With strength that is born
    of anticipation
That comes from knowing
    that autumn-time sadness
Will surely be followed
    by a springtime of gladness.

SPRING SONG

"The earth is the Lord's
 and the fulness thereof"—
It speaks of His greatness
 and sings of His love.
And the wonder and glory
 of the first Easter morn,
Like the first Christmas night
 when the Savior was born,
Are blended together
 in symphonic splendor
And God with a voice
 that is gentle and tender
Speaks to all hearts
 attuned to His voice,
Bidding His listeners
 to gladly rejoice,
For He who was born
 to be crucified
Arose from the grave
 to be glorified,
And the birds in the trees
 and the flowers of spring
All join in proclaiming
 this heavenly King.

"I Am the Light of the World"

Oh, Father, up in heaven,
    we have wandered far away
From Jesus Christ, our Savior,
    who arose on Easter Day.
And the promise of salvation
    that God gave us when Christ died
We have often vaguely questioned,
    even doubted and denied.
We've forgotten why You sent us
    Jesus Christ, Your only Son,
And in arrogance and ignorance
    it's our will, not Thine, be done.
Oh, shed Thy light upon us
    as Easter dawns this year,
And may we feel the presence
    of the risen Savior near.
And, God, in Thy great wisdom,
    lead us in the way that's right,
And may the darkness of this world
    be conquered by Thy light.

In the Garden of Gethsemane

Before the dawn of Easter
 there came Gethsemane,
Before the resurrection
 there were hours of agony.
For there can be no crown of stars
 without a cross to bear,
And there is no salvation
 without faith and love and prayer.
And when we take our needs to God
 let us pray as did His Son
That dark night in Gethsemane—
 "Thy will, not Mine, be done."

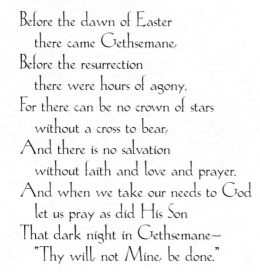

"I Know That My Redeemer Liveth"

They asked me how I know it's true
    that the Savior lived and died,
And if I believe the story
    that the Lord was crucified.
I have so many answers
    to prove His holy being,
Answers that are everywhere
    within the realm of seeing—
The leaves that fell at autumn
    and were buried in the sod
Now budding on the tree boughs
    to lift their arms to God,
The flowers that were covered
    and entombed beneath the snow
Pushing through the darkness
    to bid the spring hello—
On every side great nature
    retells the Easter story,
So who am I to question
    the resurrection glory?

THANK YOU, GOD, FOR EVERYTHING

Thank You, God, for everything—
   the big things and the small—
For every good gift comes from God,
   the giver of them all.
And all too often we accept
   without any thanks or praise
The gifts God sends as blessings
   each day in many ways.
And so at this Thanksgiving time
   we offer up a prayer

To thank You, God, for giving us
   a lot more than our share.
Thank You for the miracles
   we are much too blind to see,
And give us a new awareness
   of our many gifts from Thee,
And help us to remember
   that the key to life and living
Is to make each prayer a prayer of thanks
   and every day Thanksgiving.

THE PRICELESS GIFT
OF CHRISTMAS

Now Christmas is a season
  for joy and merrymaking,
A time for gifts and presents,
  for giving and for taking,
A festive, friendly, happy time
  when everyone is gay—
But have we ever really felt
  the greatness of the day?
For through the centuries the world
  has wandered far away
From the beauty and the meaning
  of the holy Christmas Day,
For Christmas is a heavenly gift
  that only God can give,
It's ours just for the asking,
  for as long as we shall live.
It can't be bought or bartered,
  it can't be won or sold,
It doesn't cost a penny
  and it's worth far more than gold.
It isn't bright and gleaming
  for eager eyes to see,

It can't be wrapped in tinsel
    or placed beneath a tree.
It isn't soft and shimmering
    for reaching hands to touch,
Or some expensive luxury
    you've wanted very much.
For the priceless gift of Christmas
    is meant just for the heart
And we receive it only
    when we become a part
Of the kingdom and the glory,
    which is ours to freely take,
For God sent the holy Christ Child
    at Christmas for our sake
So we might come to know Him
    and feel His presence near
And see the many miracles
    performed while He was here.
And this priceless gift of Christmas
    is within the reach of all,
The rich, the poor, the young and old,
    the greatest and the small,
So take His priceless gift of love,
    reach out and you'll receive,
And the only payment that God asks
    is just that you believe.

A New Year

What better time
and what better season,
What greater occasion
or more wonderful reason
To kneel down in prayer
and lift our hands high
To the God of creation
Who made land and sky.
And, oh, what a privilege
as the new year begins
To ask God to wipe out
our errors and sins
And to know when we ask,
if we are sincere,
He will wipe our slate clean
as we start a new year.
So at this glad season
when joy's everywhere,
Let us meet our Redeemer
at the altar of prayer.

Faith Is a Mighty Fortress

We stand once more at the end of the year
With mixed emotions of hope and fear—
Hope for the peace we long have sought,
Fear that our hopes will come to naught,
Unwilling to trust in the Father's will,
We count on our logic and shallow skill,
And in our arrogance and pride,
We are no longer satisfied
To place our confidence and love
With childlike faith in God above.
But tiny hands and tousled heads
That kneel in prayer by little beds
Are closer to the dear Lord's heart
And of His kingdom more a part
Than we who search and never find
The answers to our questioning mind,
For faith in things we cannot see
Requires a child's simplicity.
Oh, Father, grant once more to men
A simple childlike faith again,
Forgetting color, race, and creed
And seeing only the heart's deep need,
For faith alone can save our soul
And lead us to a higher goal,
For there's but one unfailing course—
We win by faith and not by force.

A Thankful Heart

Take nothing for granted,
  for whenever you do,
The joy of enjoying
  is lessened for you,
For we rob our own lives
  much more than we know
When we fail to respond
  or in any way show
Our thanks for the blessings
  that daily are ours—

The warmth of the sun,
  the fragrance of flowers,
The beauty of twilight,
  the freshness of dawn,
The coolness of dew
  on a green velvet lawn,
The kind little deeds
  so thoughtfully done,
The favors of friends
  and the love that someone
Unselfishly gives us
  in a myriad of ways,
Expecting no payment
  and no words of praise.
Oh, great is our loss
  when we no longer find
A thankful response
  to things of this kind,
For the joy of enjoying
  and the fullness of living
Are found in the heart
  that is filled with thanksgiving.

After the Winter, God Sends the Spring

Springtime is a season
   of hope and joy and cheer,
There's beauty all around us
   to see and touch and hear.
So no matter how downhearted
   and discouraged we may be,
New hope is born when we behold
   leaves budding on a tree,
Or when we see a timid flower
   push through the frozen sod
And open wide in glad surprise
   its petaled eyes to God.
For this is just God saying,
   "Lift up your eyes to Me,
And the bleakness of your spirit,
   like the budding springtime tree,
Will lose its wintry darkness
   and your heavy heart will sing" —
For God never sends the winter
   without the joy of spring.

*O*ut of My Life

Little Lights and Shadows from My Present and Past

as told by Helen Steiner Rice[1]

Not long ago I received a letter from a man who asked me what I had done to "meet life successfully." As I tried to explain to him, I am a very ordinary person. I do not think of myself as a success but as just another worker in God's vineyard. The phenomenal sale of my books and writings is not due to anything special about me or my way of living. It is a tribute to the wonderful goodness of God, not to me; at best, I am just an instrument for His message. This short account of my life has been written, at the publisher's request, not to publicize any "success secrets" but to show how completely God helps us solve our problems when we place ourselves completely in His mighty hands.

I was born in the bustling little town of Lorain, Ohio, on the shore of Lake Erie. Lorain is a busy lakeport; its steel mill is still one of the largest in the United States. Everyone in town was pretty much on an equal level socially, and my sister, Gertrude, and I had a very happy childhood.

---

[1]The recollections of her life and ministry were recorded in 1968 by Donald T. Kauffman, who was managing editor of Fleming H. Revell at the time.

My father, John A. Steiner, was a railroad engineer and a marvelous man. I never heard him swear once or lose his temper. My mother was high-spirited, but my father was always gentle and calm; he was just a very nice person. There was not an ounce of bias in him—he was as much at home with a Lake Erie fisherman as he would have been with the president. He loved to hunt, and he invited everyone from bankers to street cleaners to come hunting with him.

Mother had an exceptional flair for making lovely clothes. Everyone said that I had the most beautiful clothes in the world, and for this all the credit goes to my dear mother. She was ambitious for her children; she wanted us to be well educated and to have the better things of life. But Papa and I felt we already had everything important, and we were content with life.

When I was sixteen and a senior in high school, the bottom dropped out of my life. Papa died in a flu epidemic. Although we were not destitute, I felt that I ought to do something to help my mother and younger sister, and I started thinking about a job.[2]

I did not have to think about it long. I was offered work by the Lorain branch of the Ohio Public Service Company, first as a "pinch hitter" and then in other jobs for which I volunteered. Before long I was a director of public relations for Public Service and chairman of the women's committee on public relations for the National Electric Light Association (East Central Division).

---

[2]Helen graduated from Lorain High School on February 1, 1918, a few months before her eighteenth birthday. Her father died in October 1918. At the time of his death, Helen was already employed at the Lorain Electric Light and Power Company. After his death, however, she became the family breadwinner.

One day I was asked to speak at an electric light convention at Cedar Point. When I got to the platform I thought to myself, *I don't really know how to start this, or what to say, or even how much.* I panicked a bit—then another thought came into my mind: *Your Father knows.*

Then and there, in that split fraction of a second, I spoke to the God who means everything to me. I said, "I don't know what to do, Father—You tell me."[3]

At that moment a wonderful feeling of assurance and confidence swept over me; I knew that my heavenly Father was answering.

There were a lot of businessmen at the convention. I picked out one who looked friendly and understanding and started talking to him, and, from the response I could see in his face, I knew that what I wanted to say was getting across. Other faces started to respond, and when I finished, there was a long round of applause.

I have always spoken in public just as I would talk to someone in my living room. I never tried to make a name for myself or to use big words, so I never had the tension and struggle of getting too involved with myself. I learned to let go and let God take control.

There were many things I was anxious to speak about. Women's rights were a constant topic while I was growing up; all my teachers had been suffragettes, and I firmly believed in the right and ability of women to win their own way in the world. I developed a number of lecture topics like "Blue Eyes or Gray Matter" and "Living and Working Enthusiastically."

---

[3]Helen spoke at the Ohio Electric Light Association Convention at Cedar Point in 1924. A 1926 interview with her in *Business Magazine* indicates that she chose as her topic for the speech "Women as a Power in the Electrical Industry." It was well prepared and well received.

I discovered that many men were ready and willing to listen to an enthusiastic presentation of these matters by a blond young lady who knew how to appeal to their sense of humor as well as to their business interests and their sense of fair play.

I began receiving more and more invitations to speak. I addressed the American Electric Railway Convention (a very big thing at that time) in Washington, D.C. There I was photographed with President Calvin Coolidge. B. C. Forbes, publisher of *Forbes Magazine,* wrote me, "The place for you is not Lorain, Ohio, but some metropolitan city like New York where there is so much more room for doing big things." I had a number of statements of this kind printed in a circular, prepared a list of lecture topics, and started my own lecture circuit.

As long as I live, I'll remember the speech I made at the Statler Hotel in Buffalo, New York. (Mr. Storr, head of the Buffalo Board of Education, had read an interview with me in *Nation's Business* and had invited me to address a business luncheon at the Statler.)

When I arrived at the room where the luncheon was being held, everything was buzzing. I had never seen so many people in a room that size. I didn't know what Mr. Storr looked like, nor where I was to go; I guess I felt a little lost.

I approached a man at what looked like the head table and said, "I would like to talk to Mr. Storr."

The man replied, "You can't see him now. He's busy—he's hunting for the speaker."

I said, "I am the speaker."

The man was visibly upset. I thought he was going to collapse! He went away and returned soon with a large, imposing-looking gentleman who looked at me in such a way that if I could have shriveled up under his gaze I surely would have.

Finally he said, "There has been a mistake. We asked the woman who was photographed with President Coolidge to speak here. You are just a child!"

I was quite small and slender, and I was wearing a little gold two-piece dress with a purple toque pulled down over my forehead. At that time, dresses were very short, and Mr. Storr looked as if he thought I was a schoolgirl who had lost her way.

I said, "I'm it."

Mr. Storr tried awfully hard to be nice to me, but it was obviously a hardship. He said, "I don't think you can make yourself heard there. Have you ever talked to this many people?"

"Oh, yes," I said. "This room is really small compared to the Chamber of Commerce Hall where I spoke in Washington."

Mr. Storr said, "We've invited the whole John Larkin Company to this luncheon. John Larkin is here himself! I do hope you won't disappoint us."

What a way to build up confidence! But I asked my Father for help—as I have learned to do every time I make a speech or write a poem—and at the end of my speech Mr. Storr said, "I never would have believed you could do it." I must say that he did everything in his power to make up for the way he had greeted me. He escorted me to all the local attractions and sent me an enormous box of roses.

One evening I spoke to the Annual Clearinghouse Association of Bankers at the Dayton Country Club on the topic "Do You Know Your Job or Do You *Love* Your Job?"[4] The member delegated to meet the speaker was a tall, handsome young man named Franklin D. Rice. After the meeting, he asked me, "Would you like to go someplace and have something to eat?" Many of those present kidded me about going out with the most eligible bachelor in Dayton, Ohio.

---

[4]A newspaper account of the speech indentifies the title as "Living and Working Enthusiastically."

Franklin, I learned, had been a lieutenant in the Air Force in World War I. And when I first met him, he was an officer with the Dayton Savings and Trust Company. He commuted a great deal to New York and came from a family of outstanding ability and wealth. In a year we were married.[5]

Everyone said that I was the luckiest girl in the world, and I had to agree. For our honeymoon Franklin had arranged a cruise through the Caribbean. We had a beautiful suite on an enormous luxury liner.

About a week after the cruise began, Franklin began getting daily cablegrams from his banking associates. The stock market was beginning to fall and the Great Depression was beginning.[6] But Franklin never allowed himself to be anything but the perfect husband and host, gay and friendly to all aboard. Instead of panicking over Wall Street's crash, he followed the usually sound practice of buying while others were selling. He kept writing his bank to buy more and more stock.

For the next two years we lived more extravagantly than ever. Suspecting the truth, I wanted to let our servants go and return to work, but Franklin would not hear of it. "Do you want to advertise to the whole world that things are slipping?" he asked. "We must put up a good front no matter what happens."

Finally everything Franklin D. Rice had owned was gone. Then, one terrible gray morning, I woke up to find that Franklin was gone too. About all he left me was a note in which he had written:

---

[5]Franklin and Helen met in June 1928. They were married on January 30, 1929.

[6]The Rices honeymooned in the Carribean in February 1929. Signs of economic instability were appearing months before the stock market crashed in October 1929.

Darling, The only thing I'm sorry about is that I never could give you all the things I meant to. I hope you believe that I really wanted to give them to you, and I could have given them to you before everything went. . . . You'll always go on. I only knew one world. I just can't go down and become a bum—I have to go out with the bands playing.

After my husband's tragic death, the officers of the Gibson Company asked me to work for them.[7] When I asked what they wanted me to do, they said, "Just come and you'll find out."

The first thing they asked me to do was to make a general survey of the offices and tell them what to do to improve their greeting card business. Of course I had recommendations galore! I stylized the cards and formed various programs. Then the editor suddenly contracted pneumonia and died, and E. P. Gibson (the company's founder), his nephew J. R. Gibson, and the officers asked me to become the new editor. Although I protested that I had never written a rhyme in my life, they said, "Just take the job until we get someone."[8]

---

[7]Helen was hired by Gibson Art in December 1931. Her husband had been out of work since his bank closed at the end of 1929. To help pay off their debts, Helen at first taught bridge classes and gave motivational speeches. Finally, she agreed to work for Gibson Art in Cincinnati as a trouble shooter. She lived in a hotel during the week and visited Franklin in Dayton on weekends. Franklin, depressed over his financial situation and prolonged unemployment, committed suicide in October 1932. Helen was in Cincinnati at the time of his death.

[8]Helen had written rhymed advertisements that appeared in newspapers in the 1920s while she was working in the public utilities field. An example of her high school rhymes appears in the 1916 edition of the Lorain High School yearbook, *The Scimitar.*

There is nothing about my life that I have really planned. I am a very definite believer in the philosophy of Christ: "Consider the lilies, how they grow." I think you have to be willing to work hard and do whatever job is put before you. I don't think you can just sit down and say, "I don't want that because I want to be the head of it all." I have never been the head of anything. I always start out trying to do the job I have been given—and I always see a lot more in the job than what it had when I began it.

Still, *God's* plan is wonderful. And His timing is perfect. I always leaned toward a clear expression of faith in the cards I produced; I don't believe in keeping inside what you believe about God. He is no one to be ashamed of! But it never became possible for my poems to be published until a few years ago. I am convinced that if they had been published when I wanted them to be, they would not have found ready acceptance. *Now* is the time the world so desperately needs these messages of faith and inspiration, and people would not have responded to them previously, as they do today. The world is in such turmoil now that a great many men and women and young people are ready to listen to the message.

Millions of my poems have now been printed, and the first compilation of them ever published has sold more than 700,000 copies in less than seven years. And its seventh printing sells just as well as the newest volume off the press.

As many of my readers know, Lawrence Welk selected my poem "The Priceless Gift of Christmas" for reading on his television show, and this produced thousands of new customers for my work. That reading by Aladdin was a marvelous answer to prayer, as I pointed out in my poem "How It All Happened."

> Six years ago on *The Lawrence Welk Show*
> An artist whom so many folks know
> Received a card with a Christmas verse
> That spoke of the holy Christ Child's birth—

And for some reason it caught his eye,
And I doubt today that he even knows why.
For the reader and writer had never met,
But the writer is one who will never forget
The joyous amazement and rapt surprise
When out of the starlit Christmas skies
Across the country from shore to shore
An unknown verse never heard before
Was heard by millions of listening ears,
And the writer's dream of many years
Was answered by God in a wonderful way,
And from that night to this present day
Aladdin still reads with his magic touch
The verses that people have liked so much—
And while it may look like a happenstance,
Or something born of a lucky chance,
The writer is sure that God drew the plan
And put it into the hands of man.
And, Aladdin, one of the Lawrence Welk band,
Just carried out what the Lord had planned—
For I had prayed for many long years
Through disappointments and often tears
To find, without attempts to preach,
A way that I could somehow reach
Responsive hearts . . . much like my own
And tell them no one walks alone,
But little did I guess or know
My prayer would be answered on *The Lawrence Welk Show,*
For since "The Priceless Gift" was aired,
Through Aladdin's voice I've often shared
All the verses between these covers,
And through the years there may be others
That I can share with folks like you
For there's nothing I would rather do—
And this is the story of "How It Began"
Six years ago with "The Music Man."

A year later my poem "The Praying Hands" was read on the Welk show. Then, early in 1962, John Glenn became the first American to orbit the earth, and his remarkable testimony of faith in God inspired and delighted millions who had been thrilled by his historic flight. I composed a poem of tribute to John's mother, which was read by Aladdin that Mother's Day. John Glenn's mother wrote me:

I received your lovely poem. . . . I am so thrilled by it, I hardly know how to write to you. It is beautiful. . . . I plan to have the copy you sent to me framed, and keep it always.

From all over the world I received wonderful letters about my poems. A delegate to the United Nations took one of my books back to Bombay, and his secretary read it. She wrote me a glowing letter of appreciation, adding:

At present there is a problem about our home which I (and my parents) are most worried about and we all are most earnestly praying about it. At first, I guess, worry was a block, which made me, too, have a feeling that my prayers were not getting through. Now, even though the outcome is not evident, I am knowing, as you so well put it, "No matter in what guise or disguise things come to us, they are sent for our good from Our Father."

I just thought I would let you know how very much your letters and poems help me.

A woman in Minnesota wrote:

You are causing people to pause, weight values, and turn to the God who made us, when we need to be sustained— when our "original batteries" need recharging!

A secretary wrote of my book *Just for You:*

By the time I finished reading it, I felt as if I could move mountains, or withstand one falling on me. I wish everyone had the opportunity to read this certainly unforgettable book.

A Kentucky lady wrote:

In the past year I have read any and all of your poems I could get ahold of. Without you and your beautiful poetry to remind me constantly of God's love, I don't know where I would be—perhaps even dead—yes, even killed by my own hand. Your beautiful poetry has reminded me every hour of every day how much God cares.

You see, I have leukemia, and have a year—perhaps two— to live. And all of a sudden I was terribly frightened. I shouldn't be, I know—God was close—He had always been—and yet I felt that all of a sudden He had forgotten me.

Then—Helen Steiner Rice—I read "The End of the Road Is but a Bend in the Road," and all of a sudden I felt better. I read every poem of yours that I could get ahold of, and with each one I felt better until I'm not afraid anymore—I am closer to God than ever before, and when my time comes—I'm ready.

Another person wrote me about a cousin who was in prison:

This man had done a wrong and is paying for it at this time at the Indiana State Prison. He happens to be a cousin of mine. Since I believe in the human race I write to this man and try to encourage him. And believe you me he needs all the encouragement he can get. You may be interested to know that one way I have for doing this is to buy the most beautiful verses by Helen Steiner Rice that I can find. Not only does he get a lot of good and encouragement from these but I read and reread them myself before I send them and they give me the special lift that we all need every now and then.

I spend a lot of time replying to letters like these. Probably 75 percent of them are from people in small towns or villages, or from lonely dwellers on prairies or in apartments. A dear little grandmother wrote me that after buying my book *Just for You* she bought seven copies for her children, and then four copies for other relatives, and then six more to give to friends! She said:

> I will never get tired of reading your poems. They have brought me closer to God and have renewed my faith and given me new hope and love. I only pray every night that God will bless you with lots of good health so you can keep on writing forever and doing His work.

God does bless me with *countless* blessings. But I don't want anyone to think that I'm always happy and on top of the world. Sometimes I feel like an empty, dried-out corn husk. But, as Jimmie Davis sings, "You've got to keep on walking." Many days I say to my marvelously efficient secretary, "Mary Jo, today I feel as flat and drained out as though a ten-ton truck just ran over me. But we've got to keep going, because if we don't, we're not going to keep up with the schedule!"

Each morning before I go to my office I say this little prayer:

> Bless me, heavenly Father,
>   forgive my erring ways,
> Grant me strength to serve Thee,
>   put purpose in my days.
> Give me understanding,
>   enough to make me kind,
> So I may judge all people
>   with my heart and not my mind.
> And teach me to be patient
>   in everything I do,

Content to trust Your wisdom
and to follow after You.
And help me when I falter
and hear me when I pray
And receive me in Thy kingdom
to dwell with Thee some day.

Many times during the day I find occasion to repeat two of the lines: "Teach me to be patient" and "Help me when I falter!"

As I think back over the wonderful years I have enjoyed, I truly feel that many people are not really living—that somehow they miss the beauty and joy and goodness that God has put all around them. If my poems do anything, I believe they help people find the satisfaction of living life to its fullest. God's gifts are all around us, but so many people who receive them don't seem to be aware of them, and sometimes it seems to me that they never fully enjoy them.

Living is like breathing. I want to breathe deep so I can live! And it's possible to miss the joy of filling our lungs with fresh clean air, as well as the joy of living each moment to its fullest.

My own life has overflowed with happiness. And God has taught me the blessed secret of finding His purposes in even tragically black moments. Even the events that are unhappiest pass away and turn into things that are really wonderful. I can't waste my time thinking about things that are sad, because there are so many good things in life. Why should I dwell on the things that would only make me unhappy?

Whenever anyone thanks me for one of my books or poems, I have to give all the credit to God. I don't have much to do with these poems, really. Everything I write is borrowed—it's from God and from His age-old wisdom. I'm only an instrument for getting His message into people's lives. God gives me the ability to put it down, then He directs the traffic and gets my verse into the hands and hearts of people who find their own souls reflected in what I write.

As I said on one interview show, I have the best material in the world to work with, so nothing can compete with it! How can anyone do better than repeat the simple old words of faith and hope and kindness and love? Everything in the world may change, but these things are always valid.

Sometimes cynical people ask me what proof I have of these invisible realities I write about. What more proof could there be than what God puts all around us? Spiritual reality is like the air. You can't see it, but you can feel it, you know it is there and you couldn't live without it. I like to get up early in the morning and enjoy the wonderful songs of the birds and the smell of the flowers and trees. Then, when I walk into my office, I ask,

> Who but God could make the day
> And gently tuck the night away?

At times, I must confess, I have wondered why I had to lose my husband, Franklin, so tragically, after just the two short years we had together.[9] Only in the last three or four years have I been sure why it was permitted to happen as it did.

The night before Franklin and I were married, I told the story of a young girl who stood at the edge of a field of waving corn—a beautiful field, where every stalk was tall and green and luxuriant and every ear was perfect. And

---

[9]The Rices were married in January 1929 and Franklin died in October 1932, a period of more than three and a half years.

the farther the girl could see into the field, the larger the ears became.

A genie told the girl, "If you walk through this field, I will reward you with a gift in proportion to the size of the ear you select. There is only one restriction. You must start right where you are standing, and you may go through the field only once. You may not retrace your steps. The ear of corn you bring out will determine the reward you will receive on the other side of the field."

The girl was supremely happy as she started into the field. Carelessly she trod on many of the stalks, thinking to herself: *I won't take any of these, for in the center of the field are the most perfect ears of all. I want the biggest reward I can get.*

The girl ran on and on, intent on finding the largest ear in the field. Suddenly she realized that the corn stalks were getting smaller and thinner; she was nearing the far edge of the field. In desperation, she looked for a good ear, but she could not bring herself to pick any of those in sight. She kept thinking, *There's got to be another big ear before the end.* But there was not. She came out of the field empty-handed.

I realize now, more surely than ever before, that *things* can never bring happiness. So many people always look for something bigger and better, and as soon as they get one thing, they set their hearts on another. Happiness is, for them, a mink coat or a Cadillac—something big, something splashy. If someone shakes hands with them and says "God bless you," sincerely, they fail to realize that they have just received one of the greatest gifts there is.

If you take the love and friendship and the "God bless you's" that come your way, you have everything. The person who gets the mink coat receives nothing really worthwhile or lasting. But the true gifts of God can never be lost.

As this book nears completion, another summer of riot and bloodshed is drawing near. I have just driven through the area of Cincinnati that was ravaged and burned in a recent uprising. I looked with unbelief at the devastation and destruction so savagely done by the hand of evil, which is spreading across our country like a killing blight, and I am stunned with sadness.

There is so little that words can say at a time like this. For in these dark hours, the heart is overwhelmed with a heaviness that brings us to a closer awareness of Christ's cross. As I write, Good Friday approaches, and we can almost feel that we are walking with the Savior to our Calvary. This is not a time for words, it is a time for meditation, for our own Gethsemane.

Surely, only love can heal the sick, tired world. But God stands ready through His Son to turn this cross into a crown—if we will but let Him warm our cold hearts with His love.

I firmly believe that,

> Great is the power of might and mind,
> But only love can make us kind.
> And all we are or hope to be
> Is empty pride and vanity.
> If love is not a part of all,
> The greatest man is very small!

Yes,

> Love is the language every heart speaks
> And Love is the answer to all that man seeks.

I know that everything I have ever done is truly a gift from God. In His love I pass these gifts on from my heart to yours.[10]

---

[10]Helen went to her eternal reward on April 23, 1981.

My Thanks!

People everywhere in life
   from every walk and station,
From every town and city
   and every state and nation,
Have given me so many things
   intangible and dear,
I couldn't begin to count them all
   or even make them clear.
I only know I owe so much
   to people everywhere,
And when I put my thoughts in verse
   it's just a way to share
The musing of a thankful heart,
   a heart much like your own,
For nothing that I think or write
   is mine and mine alone.
So if you found some beauty
   in any word or line,
It's just your soul's reflection
   in proximity with mine.